Mood Trackers

26 Weekly Mood Trackers
1 Six Month Daily Tracker

On each page there is a key. Fill in the key with a color and assign a mood to it, Color in each image according to the key for each day of the week. 1 being the first day 7 being the last day.

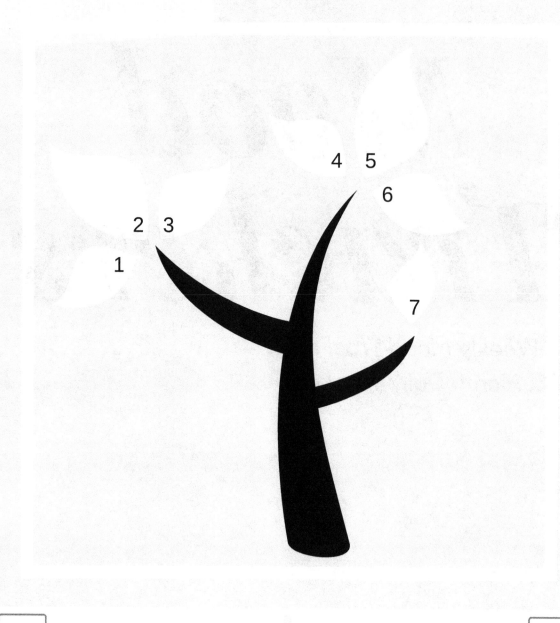

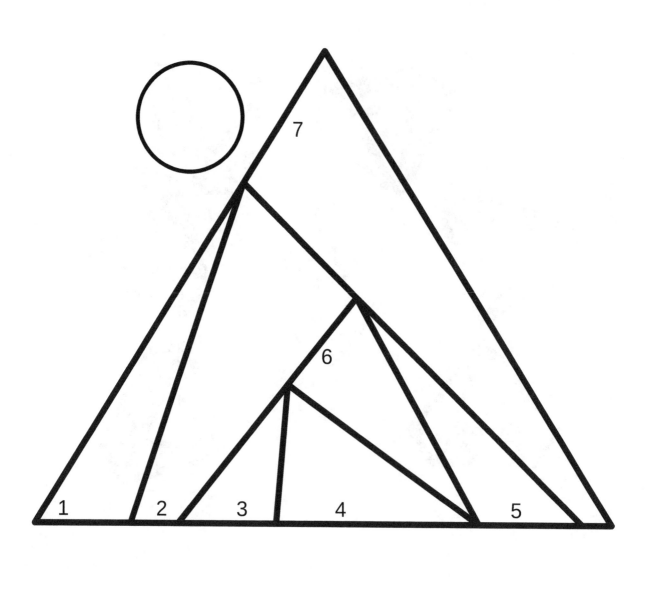

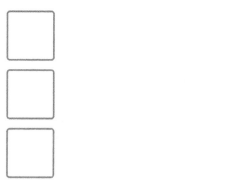

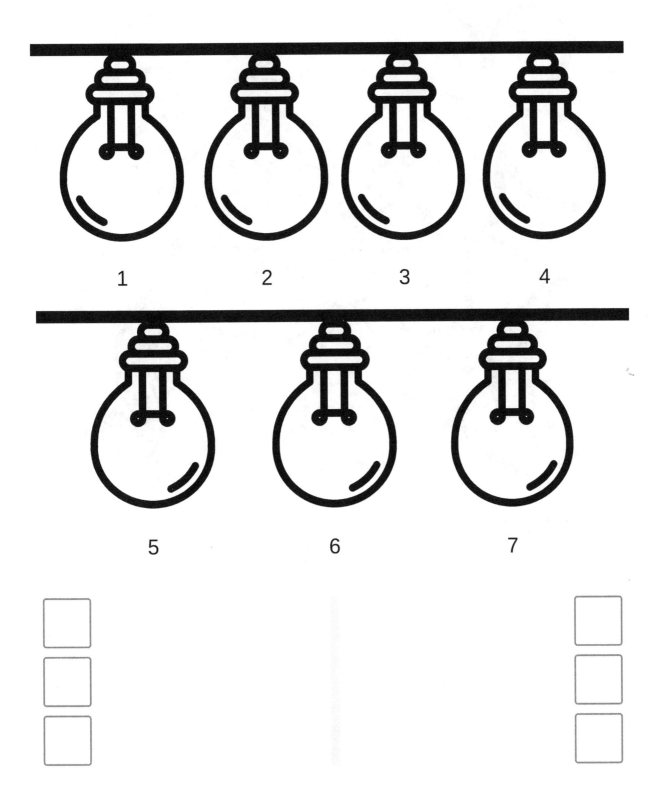

1

2

3

4

5

6

7

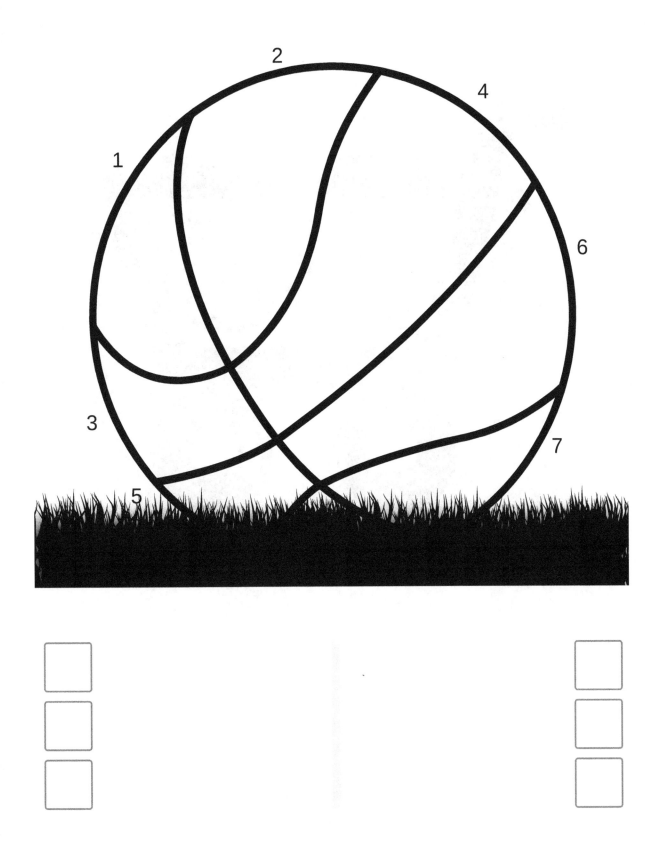

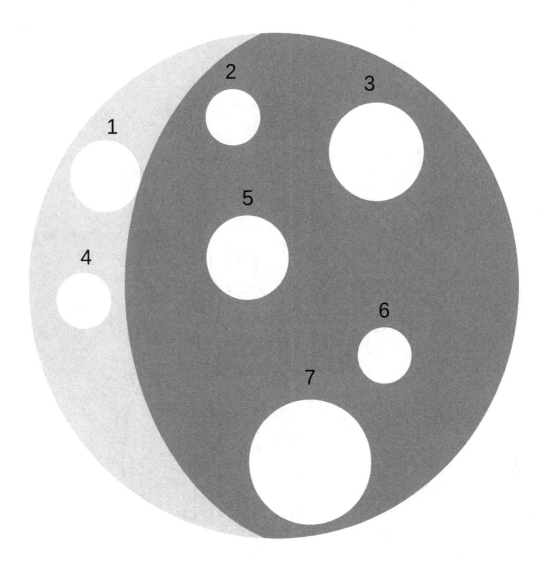

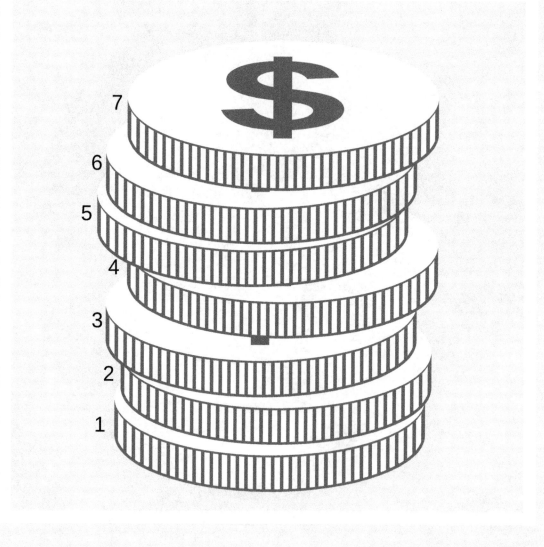

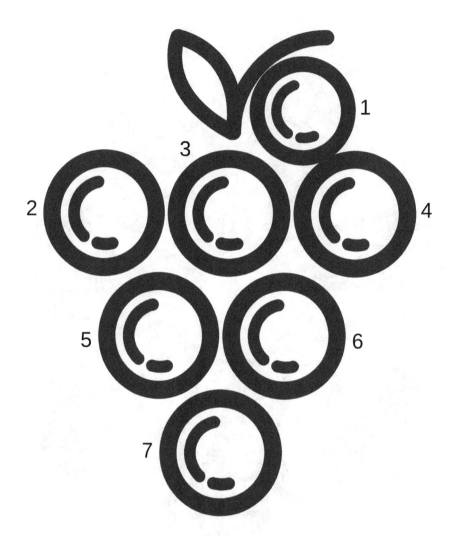

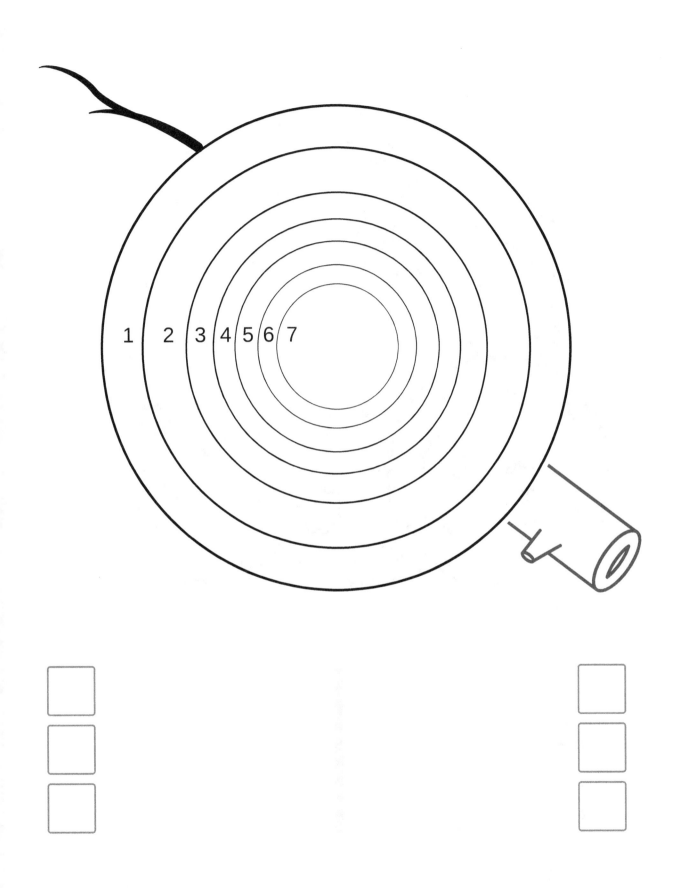

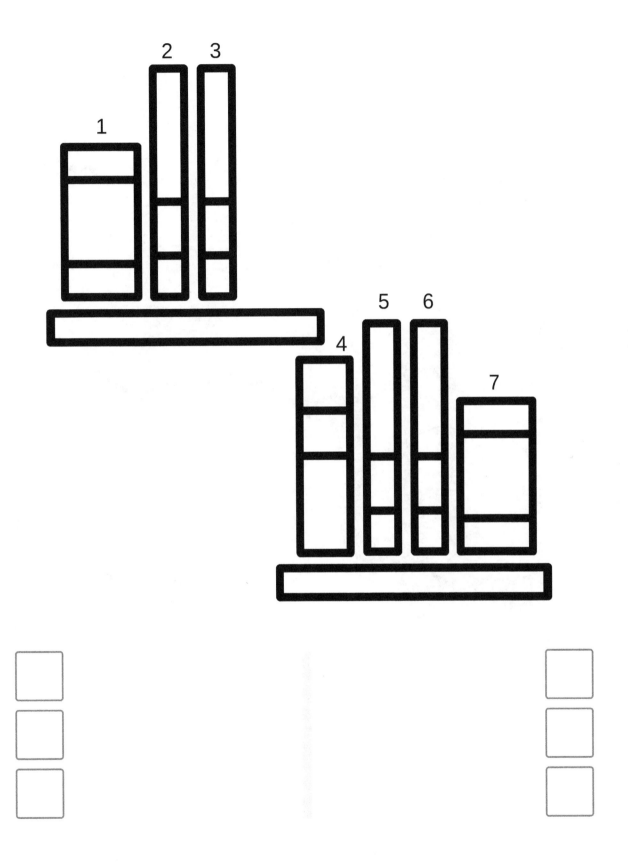

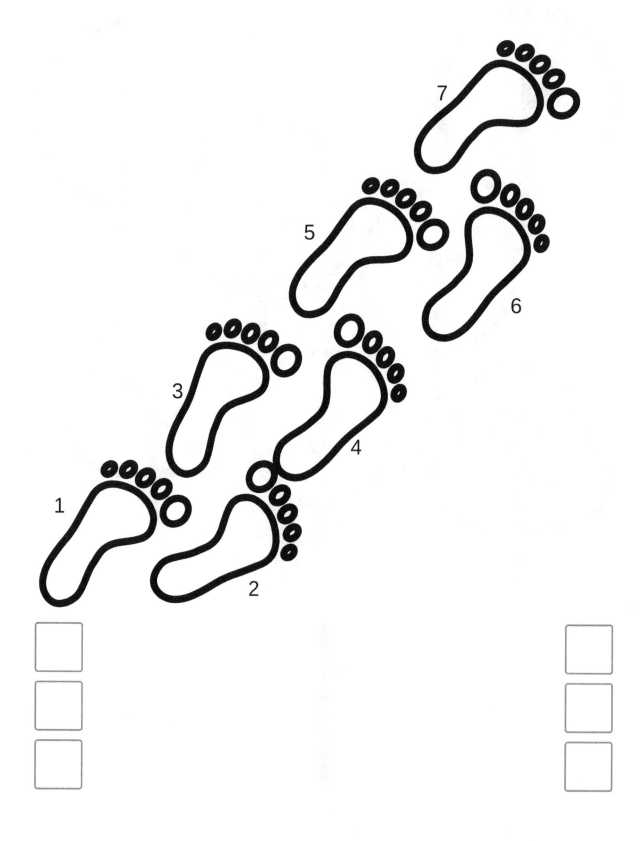

6 Months at a Glance

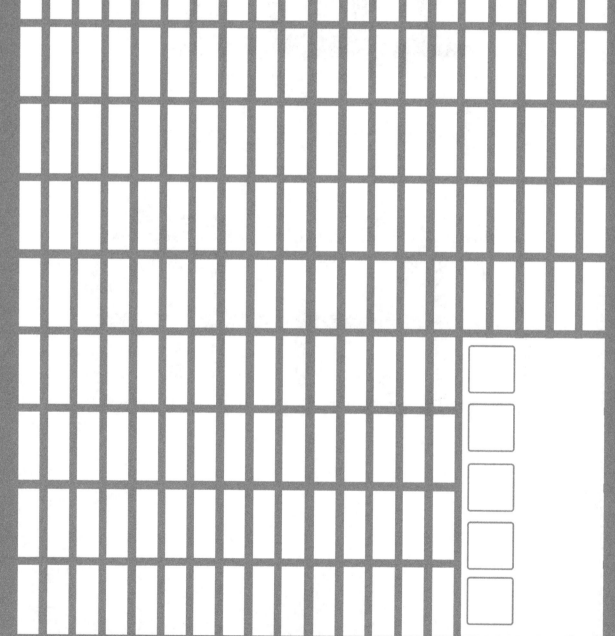

CPSIA information can be obtained
at www.ICGtesting.com
Printed in the USA
LVHW061150141019
634126LV00012B/5012/P

9 781696 793698